The Giving Bag Book Gives On...

Cara M. Hill

Halo
PUBLISHING
INTERNATIONAL

ISBN: 978-1-63765-164-3
LCCN: 2021925907

Halo Publishing International, LLC
www.halopublishing.com

Printed and bound in the United States of America

This book is dedicated to my three wonderful children Kamryn, Charlotte and Bennett.

You inspire me to be my best self, and I can only hope I do the same for you. I love you beyond words. You are all my biggest blessings.

Remember Grace, Ben and their parents? Well, do they have a story for you about one family giving to another!

They would like to introduce you to Marie, Rose, James and their parents and their neighbors, the Smiths.

The Smiths just expanded their family and welcomed a new baby!

Whether it's welcoming a new baby
or another big life event,

having a community around you is
what makes the biggest difference!

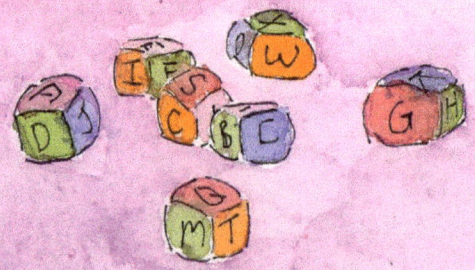

"Hey Mom, I would love to help the Smiths out by offering my time and watching Sam for them," said Marie. "Although Sam is now their oldest son, he's still a toddler."

"Hi Mrs. Smith, while Marie is watching Sam, I would love to help you out by sweeping the floors," said Rose.

"Thank you so much Rose!"
said Mrs. Smith.

James just got home from a friend's house and wondered where his sisters were. "Mom, where are Marie and Rose?" James said.

"They went to the neighbors to help since they just brought the new baby home," said Mom.

"Hmmm... I wonder what I can do to help?" said James. "I got it! I can walk their dog, Toby. Toby loves me, and I'm sure he could use the exercise," said James.

After James went next door to walk the dog, Dad got home from work.

Mom said, "Honey, how about you mow the Smith's lawn while I finish up this casserole for them?"

So, you see, this entire family gave something, and it wasn't a thing at all!

Let's not forget that not only can we give our toys and clothes, but we can also give of ourselves, our time and our hearts.

Parents, let's talk.

*What is giving?

*Why should we give?

*Who benefits when we give?

Give On!!!

www.ingramcontent.com/pod-product-compliance
Lightning Source LLC
LaVergne TN
LVHW070839080426
835511LV00025B/3485

9 781637 651643